Searchlight
BOOKS

How
Do Simple
Machines Work?

Put
Inclined
Planes
to the Test

by Sally M. Walker and Roseann Feldmann

Lerner Publications Company
Minneapolis

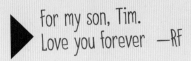

For my son, Tim.
Love you forever —RF

Lerner Publications Company
A division of Lerner Publishing Group, Inc.
241 First Avenue North
Minneapolis, MN 55401 U.S.A.

Website address: www.lernerbooks.com

Library of Congress Cataloging-in-Publication Data

Walker, Sally M.
        Put inclined planes to the test / by Sally M. Walker and Roseann Feldmann.
             p.   cm. — (Searchlight books™—How do simple machines work?)
        Includes index.
        ISBN 978-0-7613-5324-9 (lib. bdg. : alk. paper)
        1. Inclined planes—Juvenile literature. I. Feldmann, Roseann. II. Title.
    TJ147.W345 2012
    621.8—dc22   2009032228

Manufactured in the United States of America
1 – DP – 7/15/11

Contents

Chapter 1

WORK

You work every day. You work when you walk up the stairs.

Walking up the stairs is work. What are other examples of work?

You work when you climb a ladder. It may surprise you to learn that playing is work too.

Playing baseball is work!

Work = Using Force to Move an Object

When scientists use the word *work*, they don't mean the opposite of play. Work is using force to move an object from one place to another. Force is a push or a pull. You use force to do chores and to play.

You use force when you lift a box.

This girl is moving a container from one place to another, so she is doing work.

Sometimes you push or pull an object to move it to a new place. Then you have done work. The distance that the object moves may be long or short. But the object must move.

Pulling a Sled Is Work

Pulling a sled uphill is work. Your force moves the sled to the top of the hill.

You use force when you pull your sled up a hill. You are doing work.

But Pushing a Building Isn't Work

Pushing a building is not work. It's not work if you sweat. It's not work even if you push until your arms feel like rubber. No matter how hard you try, you have not done work. The building has not moved. If the building moves, then you have worked!

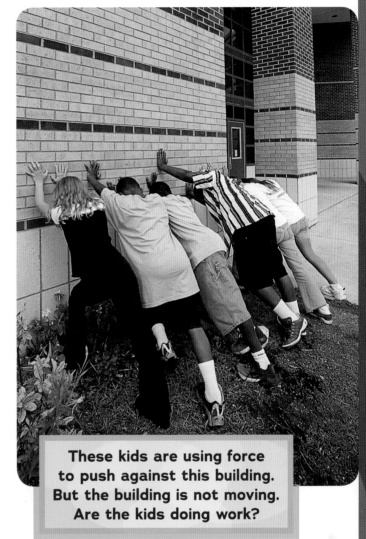

These kids are using force to push against this building. But the building is not moving. Are the kids doing work?

Chapter 2

MACHINES

Most people want to make doing work easier. Machines are tools that make work easier. Some of them make work go faster too.

A bulldozer is a machine with many moving parts. What do we call machines with many moving parts?

Complicated Machines

Some machines have many moving parts. We call them complicated machines. It may be hard to understand how complicated machines work. Escalators and bulldozers are complicated machines.

An escalator is a complicated machine.

Simple Machines

Some machines are easy to understand. They are called simple machines. Simple machines have few moving parts.

A staircase is a simple machine.

Simple machines are found in every home, school, and playground. They are so simple that most people don't realize they are machines.

A doorknob has few moving parts. It is a simple machine.

Chapter 3

WHAT IS AN INCLINED PLANE?

An inclined plane is a simple machine. An inclined plane is a flat surface. One end is higher than the other. Using an inclined plane makes it easier to lift or lower heavy objects.

This girl is using an inclined plane. What kind of machine is an inclined plane?

Experiment Time

You can prove this for yourself. You'll need five or six thick books, a heavy weight, and the board from a family game. The heavy weight might be a 5-pound (2-kilogram) bag of flour. Or you could use a very large can of food.

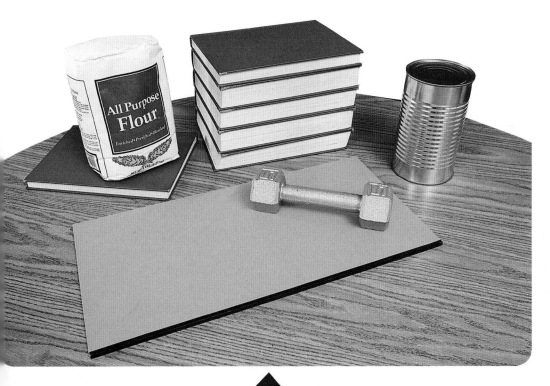

YOU CAN SHOW THAT AN INCLINED PLANE MAKES WORK EASIER. THESE ARE THE THINGS YOU WILL NEED.

Stack the books on a table. Put the weight next to the books. Try to lift the weight up onto the books with one hand. Use two hands if you have to. Lift it several times. Lifting the weight straight up takes a lot of force.

It takes a lot of force to lift a heavy object by yourself.

Next, lean the game board against the books. The game board should be folded in half. The top end of the board should be near the edge of the top book. You have turned the board into an inclined plane.

Place another book on the high edge of the game board. The book will help keep the board in place.

Slide the weight up the inclined plane. You can probably do this with just one hand. Pushing the weight up the inclined plane is easier than lifting it. Pushing takes less force than lifting the weight straight up.

An inclined plane makes it easier to move a heavy object to a higher place.

How Much Force?

This girl is lifting a picnic basket to the top of a fort. The basket is heavy, so she must use a lot of force. How much force is she using to lift the basket?

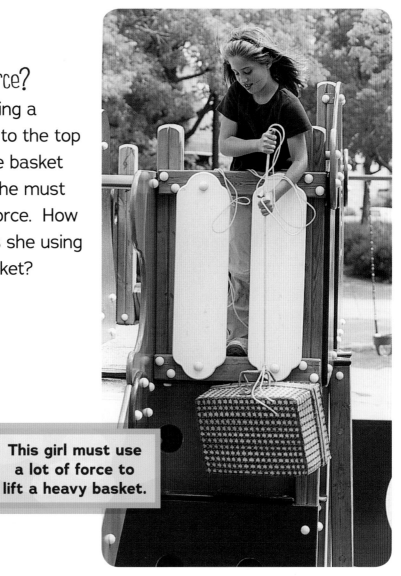

This girl must use a lot of force to lift a heavy basket.

Here the basket is hanging from a spring scale. A spring scale measures force. This spring scale is measuring how much force the girl is using to lift the basket.

The girl is using about 17 units of force to lift the basket.

This time, the girl tries something new. She uses the slide as an inclined plane. She puts the basket on the bottom of the slide. Then she pulls it up the slide. The spring scale shows that the girl is using less force. Pulling the basket up the slide is easier than lifting it.

The girl pulled the basket a longer distance. But her work was easier. She used less force.

Here the girl is using about 7 units of force.

This person is climbing a ladder. The ladder is the shortest distance from a low place to a high place. But the climber must use a lot of force to get to the top.

A straight ladder is the shortest distance from a low place to a high place. But a climber must use a lot of force.

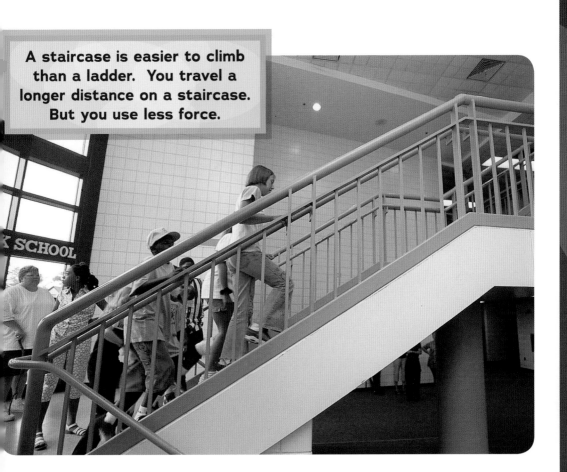

A staircase is easier to climb than a ladder. You travel a longer distance on a staircase. But you use less force.

A staircase is an inclined plane. Climbing a staircase is easier than climbing a ladder. The climber travels a longer distance. But climbing each step takes less force. The inclined plane makes it easier for the climber to get to a higher place.

Chapter 4

GRAVITY AND FRICTION

An inclined plane makes it easier to move an object from a high place to a low place. You can prove it.

Cans tumble down an inclined plane at a recycling center. How is the inclined plane helping in this case?

Experiment Time Again!

Put the heavy weight onto the pile of books. Lower it back down to the table. Lower the weight several times. Lowering the weight back to the table takes a lot of force.

It takes a lot of force to lower a heavy object.

Next, push the weight up the board. When the weight is near the top, let go. What happens?

PUSH YOUR WEIGHT TO THE TOP
OF YOUR INCLINED PLANE.

The weight slides back down the inclined plane. You don't have to push it. The inclined plane made it easy to lower the weight back to the table. Why was it so easy?

Gravity made it easy to lower the weight. Gravity is a force that pulls objects toward the ground. Gravity pulled the weight down the inclined plane.

An inclined plane makes it easy to lower a heavy object. Gravity pulls an object down an inclined plane.

A hill is an inclined plane. A snow-covered hill is great for sledding. Gravity pulls the sled downhill. But another force acts on the sled too. The other force is called friction. Friction is a force that stops or slows moving objects.

Gravity pulls a sled down a snowy hill.

There isn't much friction between two smooth surfaces. A surface is the outside of an object. Icy, packed snow and the bottom of a sled are both smooth. There isn't much friction between them. So a sled slides easily on packed snow. There would be a lot of friction between a sled and grass. The friction between them would stop the sled from moving. That's why people don't sled on grassy hills.

There isn't much friction between a sled and the snow on a hill. So the sled slides easily down the hill.

Now Try This

Put your heavy weight on the top end of the game board and let go. The weight slides fast because the board is smooth. There isn't much friction between the board and the weight. The smooth board helps the weight slide quickly, the same way snow helps a sled slide.

There isn't much friction between the weight and the game board. The weight slides easily.

A towel will change the amount of friction on your inclined plane.

How could you change the amount of friction on your inclined plane? Put a bath towel on the game board. Try sliding the weight down. How fast does it slide?

The weight probably didn't slide at all. Or maybe it slid very slowly. The surface of a towel is bumpy. There is a lot of friction between the towel's bumpy surface and the weight. There is enough friction to slow or stop the weight, the same way grass would stop a sled.

Friction can stop a heavy object from sliding down an inclined plane.

A ramp is an inclined plane. Some ramps are smooth. Their slippery surface does not have much friction. It is easy to slide a weight up or down a smooth ramp. It is much easier than moving a weight straight up or down.

An inclined plane makes doing work easier. Traveling a longer distance lets a person use less force. A person can use even less force going down an inclined plane because gravity helps.

MOVING VAN

smooth ramp

MOVING VAN

smooth ramp

The movers don't need to use much force to push their boxes on these smooth ramps. But one of the movers is using less force than the other. Do you know which one it is?

Chapter 5

INCLINED PLANES ARE EVERYWHERE

Inclined planes are all around us. We use them every day to make our work easier.

Dump truck beds are inclined planes. The beds can be tilted to dump out a load.

This dump truck's bed is an inclined plane. What's another everyday example of an inclined plane?

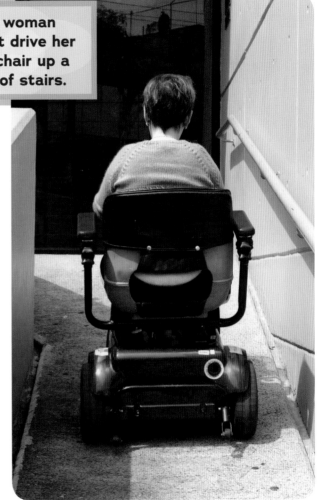

This woman couldn't drive her wheelchair up a flight of stairs.

Wheelchair ramps are inclined planes. They help people in wheelchairs get into buildings.

Roads are inclined planes. They let us drive up mountains and steep hills.

Getting up a mountain would be hard work without the help of an inclined plane.

Slanted roofs are inclined planes. They help water or snow slide off the roof.

Using inclined planes gives you an advantage. An advantage is a better chance of finishing your work.

Using an inclined plane is almost like having a helper. And that's a real advantage!

Slanted roofs give people an advantage. They get snow and rain off the roof so homeowners don't have to clean their roofs as often.

Glossary

complicated machine: a machine that has many moving parts

force: a push or a pull

friction: a force that stops or slows moving objects

gravity: a force that pulls objects toward the ground

inclined plane: a flat surface with one end higher than the other

simple machine: a machine that has few moving parts

work: moving an object from one place to another

Learn More about Simple Machines

Books

Christiansen, Jennifer. *Get to Know Inclined Planes*. New York: Crabtree Publishing Company, 2009. Find out more about inclined planes and how we use them.

Gosman, Gillian. *Inclined Planes in Action*. New York: PowerKids Press, 2011. See examples of inclined planes and how they work.

Walker, Sally M., and Roseann Feldmann. *Put Wedges to the Test*. Minneapolis: Lerner Publications Company, 2012. Read all about wedges, another important simple machine.

Way, Steve, and Gerry Bailey. *Simple Machines*. Pleasantville, NY: Gareth Stevens, 2009. This title explores a variety of simple machines, from wheels and axles to ramps and levers.

Websites

Edheads: Simple Machines Activities
http://www.edheads.org/activities/simple-machines
Learn about simple and complicated machines as you play games and explore a house and a toolshed.

Quia—Simple Machines
http://www.quia.com/quiz/101964.html
Visit this site to find a challenging interactive quiz that allows budding physicists to test their knowledge of simple machines.

Simple Machines
http://sln.fi.edu/qa97/spotlight3/spotlight3.html
This website features brief information about simple machines and helpful links you can click on to learn more.

Index

Photo Acknowledgments

Photographs copyright © Andy King. Additional images are used with the permission of: © Amy Myers/Dreamstime.com, p. 5; © Seymour Hewitt/Iconica/Getty Images, p. 8; © Stephen Mcsweeny/ Shutterstock Images, p. 10; © Leung Cho Pan/Dreamstime.com, p. 11; © Lyn Balzer and Tony Perkins/ Stone/Getty Images, p. 22; © Visions of America/SuperStock, p. 24; © Mehmet Dilsiz/Dreamstime. com, p. 28; © Intst/Dreamstime.com, p. 29; © Laura Westlund/Independent Picture Service, p. 33; © Zacarias Pereira Da Mata/Dreamstime.com, p. 34; © iStockphoto.com/Andres Balcazar, p. 35; © Kushnirov Avraham/Dreamstime.com, p. 36; © Mark Hryciw/Dreamstime.com, p. 37.

Front cover: © Charles Aghoian/Dreamstime.com.

Main body text set in Adrianna Regular 14/20.
Typeface provided by Chank.